MW00931563

This notebook belongs to:

____

Accountant Life Publishing

Made in the USA
Las Vegas, NV
24 November 2024

12533488R00066